A Garland of Poems
for Christmas

A Garland of Poems
for Christmas

compiled by Martyn Crucefix
and Michael Glover

1889 books

A Garland of Poems for Christmas

Copyright © 2022

Cover © 1889 books.
Painting of garland on cover courtesy of Ruth Dupré

www.1889books

ISBN: 978-1-915045-11-9

Dedications

*For Christmases past, present and yet to come –
with love to Louise*   – Martyn

*For my treasured Ruth, whose lovely flower garland
adorns the cover*   – Michael

Contents

Michael Glover: Uncontrollable Mysteries

Martyn Crucefix: Four Calling Birds

i/ Mother and Child

ii / Hearth and Home

iii / Far and Near

iv / Light and Sound

Uncontrollable Mysteries

chosen by Michael Glover

The Very First Poem of Christmas
(and others following after...)

Perhaps it is rank folly to ask when the very first Christmas poem was written. Who could ever possibly know? And what is a poem anyway? And the idea of Christmas comes burdened with a multitude of vexations of its own, too. Are we talking about the arduous simplicities of a birth in an inhospitable place half a world away a couple of millennia ago, or the Christmas of later fabrications, Germanic, Scandinavian, or English-Victorian? We will try in this selection to encompass a little bit of much of this in order to please as many as possible...

Some would argue that the very first Christmas poem is the prologue to the gospel by that beloved disciple St John. Given that it was written in a prose of such beauty, gravity and exaltedness, does it not deserve to be christened poetry? Prose poetry? There is nothing of the nitty-gritty earthiness of actually giving birth about it, of course....

In the beginning was the Word, and the Word was with God, and the Word was God. The same was in the beginning with God. All things were made by him; and without him was not anything made that was made. In him was life; and the life was the light of men. And the Light shineth in darkness; and the darkness comprehended it not...

According to Constant Mews, a world expert on Peter Abelard, the earliest Christmas poem is likely to be 'Jesu refulsit omnium' by St Hilary of Poitiers (c.315-367). 'Carols have been sung to celebrate Christmas since the fourth century when Christians first took over the Roman feast of the sun to celebrate the birth of the Saviour. *Jesus refulsit omnium* would have been sung at Lauds on the feast of the Epiphany,' he writes.

Here are the first three verses of the Latin original, followed by a version in English by the poet Hilary Davies, together with her own commentary.

1

Jesus Refulsit Omnium

Jesus refulsit omnium
Pius redemptor gentium
Totum genus fidelium
Laudes celebret dramatum

Quem stella natum fulgida
Monstrat micans per authera
Magosque duxit praevia
Ipsius ad cunabula

Illi cadentes parvulum
Pannis adorant obsitum
Verum fatentur ut Deum
Munus ferendo mysticum.

St Hilary of Poitiers

Jesus shines, light to all peoples,
Loving redeemer of mankind
Let all who seek him
Sing his praises, tell his story.

The glittering star,
Floating in the heavens,
Shows his cradle,
Draws the wise men on.

They kneel to adore
The child wrapped in rags
Announcing here true God
With their holy gifts.

The oldest Christmas poem that has come down to us is also by tradition the oldest Christmas hymn. It is attributed to St. Hilary of Poitiers, a Christian convert at the end of the pagan world. He knew Greek, and was well-read in the classical authors. Travelling tirelessly across France, Italy and the eastern Mediterranean in an era when the fastest transport was boat and horse, he argued with emperors, influenced saints, and founded what is generally regarded as the oldest working monastery in France.

It is only the first three stanzas that deal with the Christmas narrative. Hilary bases himself on the account of the visit of the Magi in Matthew 2: 9-12. The star is consciously guiding the wise men to this unlikely destination. The star, we also see, is Christ himself, which represents a bold conflation of two ideas of light. Matthew, however, makes no mention of an inn, stable or manger. Drawing almost certainly on the Lucan account of the humbleness of Christ's birth makes Hilary one of the very earliest to combine these two nativity stories: the majesty of the wise men with their gifts fit for a king, and the disconcertingly modest nature of their recipient. All earthly expectations of glory and power are being here overturned…

Behold A Silly Tender Babe

BEHOLD a silly tender Babe,
In freezing winter night,
In homely manger trembling lies
Alas! a piteous sight.

The inns are full, no man will yield
This little Pilgrim bed;
But forced He is with silly beasts
In crib to shroud His head.

Despise Him not for lying there,
First what He is inquire;
An orient pearl is often found
In depth of dirty mire.

Weigh not His crib, His wooden dish,
Nor beasts that by Him feed;
Weigh not His mother's poor attire,
Nor Joseph's simple weed.

This stable is a prince's court,
This crib His chair of state;
The beasts are parcel of His pomp,
The wooden dish His plate.

With joy approach, O Christian Wight!
Do homage to thy King;
And highly praise this humble pomp
Which He from heaven doth bring.

Robert Southwell (1561-1595)

The Birth

All that needs to be done shall be done.
With the single star standing over,
Solemnity will attend upon the presentation
Of the treasures by the potentates.

Meanwhile, shepherds will blink awake
In the night, and a certain fearsome glory
Will lead them hurryingly down,
Stubbing their bleeding toes as they stumblingly go,

To a cow byre's homely stink, where a bundled child
Will have the fine-wrought shells of its tiny ears
Cocked to multitudes in the God-gracious heavens above,
Which shall be daubed all over with singing.

Michael Glover

The Magi

Now as at all times I can see in the mind's eye,
In their stiff, painted clothes, the pale, unsatisfied ones
Appear and disappear in the blue depths of the sky.
With all their ancient faces like rain-beaten stones,
And all their helms of silver hovering side by side,
And all their eyes still fixed, hoping to find once more
The uncontrollable mystery on the bestial floor.

W.B.Yeats (1865-1939)

The Kiss

I see the mother, wearied, and still
hurting, lean in over the child new-born,
and kiss his lips, so gently so
wonder-fully, cherishing the baby-scent
from that damp flesh, the touch of clay
of the good earth; moment of woman
greeting cosmos, of cosmos calling
to its Creator, kiss of earth and heaven.

There will be the caress of the child –
from the mountain high to the slaughter-
table of the lamb, from the unformulated
palette of the sloblands to the skein
of geese come wheeling and crying
through suburban dusk. . .
                              And I see
a wilderness of tents across infertile
ground, scattered like sheets blown down
off a clothes-line, the women's kaftans
blowing in a desert wind, while a child
sits in the dirt, flies at his lips and nostrils.

Look! God-with-us tramps the swampy
washed-away ditches with the Rohingya
Muslim refugee of Myanmar who bears
the perishable child-Yeshua in his arms
and gazes up bewildered towards the sky
of a foreign land.
                              See how we are blessed,
returning with the host that has scarcely
grazed our lips, and though you and I
are ageing, we can offer to each other
the kiss of mutual trust and surrender.

Listen! Yeshua-child snores softly,
wrapped in a blue-wool blanket on the bench
beside a stubborn old down-and-out
who is snoring loudly; you will know love,
the way you can accept the kiss of froth
when the wave is spent beneath your feet,
and perhaps, at the end, at the forgetting,
you'll cherish the kiss of the Child on your cold
and colder lips.
                So lullay lullay then thou little
tiny child, thy mother's breast awaits
to nourish thee, thy father's arms to gentle thee,
his robe to shelter thee from the wild winds.

John F. Deane (1946-)

Christmas by the Seaside

Terrible festival happiness of the cosy eaters
who have built a blinkered ark against the waters of war
and who, rising from the table, draw curtains over their minds
lest brains should be keener and lighter
        than hearts and stomachs are.

Unconsciously pitiful the artless limbs of the child,
moving frilly-encumbered round a festooned Christmas tree,
embryo woman form, potential of thoughtful beauty:
creature already cluttered with a tinsel destiny.

Outside in the black world beyond the snug harbour
the terrible killing continues, but inside the thin pity
has been so diminished by custom and rehearsal
it has become irritation at the radio voice from the city.

Surely, surely the anguish and the exquisite hope
of life that is stauncher than flesh and domestic emotion
are implicit in the surf and the spray and the disturbing stranger,
the skeleton at the feast, the ghost thrown up by the ocean?

Phyllis Shand Allfrey (1908-86)

The Nativity of Our Lord
and Saviour Jesus Christ

Where is this stupendous stranger,
Swains of Solyma, advise?
Lead me to my Master's manger,
Show me where my Saviour lies.

O Most Mighty! O Most Holy!
Far beyond the seraph's thought,
Art thou then so mean and lowly
As unheeded prophets taught?

O the magnitude of meekness!
Worth from worth immortal sprung;
O the strength of infant weakness,
If eternal is so young!

If so young and thus eternal,
Michael tune the shepherd's reed,
Where the scenes are ever vernal,
And the loves be Love indeed!

See the God blasphem'd and doubted
In the schools of Greece and Rome;
See the pow'rs of darkness routed,
Taken at their utmost gloom.

Nature's decorations glisten
Far above their usual trim;
Birds on box and laurels listen,
As so near the cherubs hymn.

Boreas now no longer winters
On the desolated coast;
Oaks no more are riv'n in splinters
By the whirlwind and his host.

Spinks and ouzels sing sublimely,
"We too have a Saviour born;"
Whiter blossoms burst untimely
On the blest Mosaic thorn.

God all-bounteous, all-creative,
Whom no ills from good dissuade,
Is incarnate, and a native
Of the very world He made.

Christopher Smart (1722-1771)

The Burning Babe

As I in hoary winter's night stood shivering in the snow,
Surpris'd I was with sudden heat which made my heart to glow;
And lifting up a fearful eye to view what fire was near,
A pretty Babe all burning bright did in the air appear;
Who, scorched with excessive heat, such floods of tears did shed
As though his floods should quench his flames
                which with his tears were fed.
"Alas!" quoth he, "but newly born, in fiery heats I fry,
Yet none approach to warm their hearts or feel my fire but I!
My faultless breast the furnace is, the fuel wounding thorns,
Love is the fire, and sighs the smoke,
                the ashes shame and scorns;
The fuel Justice layeth on, and Mercy blows the coals,
The metal in this furnace wrought are men's defiled souls,
For which, as now on fire I am to work them to their good,
    So will I melt into a bath to wash them in my blood."
    With this he vanish'd out of sight and swiftly shrunk away,
    And straight I called unto mind that it was Christmas day.

Robert Southwell (1561-1595)

Lark-Song, Leaf-Fall

I watched the leaf, gold-sycamore, in its slow glissando
down the skyways to the brown
earth;

but words for the Christ-birth, for the infant God's
drop onto our fallen world I could not
negotiate,

this child nestling, this insomniac moon, the hard matter
of the globe against which we knock
our bones.

The sounding-board of heather bogland makes the cries
of meadow-pipit, snipe and curlew
ring,

and the lark, sky-high so that you see, and see again, lose
it, but hear its trills and halleluiahs,
its exulting

until soon the lark descending stirs you, its slow inclining,
its flub and lapsing, down to the hidden nest,
still point,

the heart beating. We grow from crib to cross, from crib
through cross. . . In the manger, look! the baby's
reaching, see

his screwed-up features, as yet the hard-won flight of the Christ
is scarce forethought of. Consult the beasts
again:

the heavy-headed ox, the lumpen soft-hearted ewe, consult, too,
the assaulted woman in intensive care,
the man

stretched sodden-hearted in the stench of an alleyway. . .
what words for these? what Word? Finches
in their charms,

eagles in their convocations: descent of the Godhead
into the secret nest. . .
therefore –

hush, hush, at last, the babe, dutifully, sleeps.

John F. Deane (1946-)

Dreamer

A sultry night;
he sits outside, young father,
head against the gable wall, and dreams, dreams
the baby, refugee, housed in a cardboard box, suffering

the tyranny
of men; wakes, chafed
by the stone. So many stars, who could credit it?
Silence from the birth-room. Settles himself, dreams –

the grey-black night
is falling to shards of deep
darkness, storms clamouring through trees
where huge black birds come out of darkness to roost.

He wakes,
body aching, sweat on his face,
and hears a cry, like a lamb's, hears the woman
softly – *hush-hush, Yeshua child, hush.* The new world,

dawn will be
a stable-door opening
onto light, bringing difficult demands,
of love, justice, and peace. He goes in; the newborn,

face creased
in distaste, holds a seed
of bitterness under the tongue; the mother,
rocking, is watchful. He lights a stove; heats a little

olive oil, slices
an onion, chops tomatoes and
crushes garlic cloves, slices a lemon, adds
herbs and spices. He fries and stirs, breaks in an egg,

then fries
a generous lamb cutlet; when he
turns towards the woman, she smiles, and he
hands her the dish. It will do, he thinks, yes, it will do.

John F. Deane (1946-)

Christmas Eve

Lemons, say two, with the garlic she wanted –
What else could bring the British out of bed
to the wind-tossed planets, the stumbled street,
but Christmas, that shared ache inside the head?

The old car rides the road's humps, patiently.
I shiver the car park's plain of frost, then see
sprouts tower, ringed by garlic. And lemons. Say three.

Alison Brackenbury (1953-)

from: **Ode on the Morning of Christ's Nativity**

This is the month, and this the happy morn,
    Wherein the Son of Heav'n's eternal King,
Of wedded Maid, and Virgin Mother born,
      Our great redemption from above did bring;
      For so the holy sages once did sing,
         That he our deadly forfeit should release,
         And with his Father work us a perpetual peace.
...

But peaceful was the night
Wherein the Prince of Light
    His reign of peace upon the earth began:
The winds with wonder whist,
Smoothly the waters kist,
    Whispering new joys to the mild Ocean,
Who now hath quite forgot to rave,
While birds of calm sit brooding on the charmed waves.
...

Ring out ye crystal spheres!
Once bless our human ears
    (If ye have power to touch our senses so)
And let your silver chime
Move in melodious time,
    And let the bass of Heav'n's deep organ blow;
And with your ninefold harmony
Make up full consort to th'angelic symphony.

John Milton (1608-1674)

Christmas

Awake, glad heart! Get up and sing,
It is the birthday of thy King,
   Awake! Awake!
   The sun doth shake
Light from his locks, and all the way
Breathing perfumes, doth spice the day.

Awake, awake! Hark, how the wood rings,
Winds whisper, and the busy springs
   A consort make;
   Awake, awake!
Man is their high-priest, and should rise
To offer up the sacrifice.

I would I were some bird or star,
Fluttering in woods, or lifted far
   Above this inn
   And road of sin!
Then either star, or bird, should be
Shining, or singing still to Thee.

I would I had in my best part
Fit rooms for Thee! Or that my heart
   Were so clean as
   Thy manger was!
But I am all filth, and obscene,
Yet if Thou wilt, Thou canst make clean.

Sweet Jesu! will then; Let no more
This leper haunt, and soil Thy door,
   Curse him, ease him
   O release him!
And let once more by mystic birth
The Lord of life be born in earth.

Henry Vaughan (1622-1695)

from: **Unto Us a Child is Born**

Celestial fowlis in the air,
Sing with your notis upon hight,
In firthis and in forestis fair
Be mirthful now at all your might;
For passed is your dully night,
Aurora has the cloudis perst,
The Son is risen with gladsum light,
Et nobis Puer natus est.

William Dunbar (c.1460-c.1520)

My mother's mother does something unexpected

Were old beliefs her charm or flaw?
No hawthorn brushed her guarded door.
One Christmas fly

brought good luck, cherished. Had mild spells
let them eke out their hoarded coals?
But now, a fly

would land unnoticed. Loud bees go
through hot December, roses blow.
They praised their fly,

reached, through ferocious cleanliness,
a glow to which small wings drew, blessed.
Flushed blue, one fly

brings, to my kitchen, buzz of sky.
The well-brushed feet, lit domes of eye
now watch me scribble, humbled by
my Christmas fly.

Alison Brackenbury (1953-)

There is a widespread superstition in Britain that it is unlucky to bring hawthorn blossom – 'may' – into the house. Amy Mary Wright, my mother's other, began meeting 'the Christmas fly' in Buckinghamshire in the 1890s – and was still encouraging its Lincolnshire cousins in the 1960s...

Trading Places

rain down, you heavens, from above

The way up into the hayloft was a wooden ladder
cruel with splinters; it rose
rough-hewn and steep, out of the stable, cows snuffling

in bulked contentment, and lowing softly; above
in a fragrant gloom, hay dust tickled me
into satisfying sneezes. I lay back, alert and absent,

lazing between earth and heaven, watched the wraiths
and angels in the rafters,
imaginary mouths unspeaking, bats above them, twitching
their black-silk presences. Morning, I was slop-sloshing
water, yard-brushing dung out under the rains.
Near midnight I heard – ringing from the choir-loft – *rorate coeli*

desuper et nubes fluant justum. I knelt before the manger, sensing
that everything – moon, kneeler, a mistle-thrush's
tracks on the snow – was now more than ever it had been, peace

possible amongst us, tenderness, and love. The Word
had wakened into the being of our world,
the unspeakable become verb, translatable. Language become

humanity's return to divinity, the infant's high-register cries,
the syrinx of a singing bird, all
framing one sentence, a staircase rising towards the heavens.

John F. Deane (1946-)

Christmas

After all pleasures as I rid one day,
My horse and I, both tired, body and mind,
With full cry of affections, quite astray;
I took up the next inn I could find.

There when I came, whom found I but my dear,
My dearest Lord, expecting till the grief
Of pleasures brought me to Him, ready there
To be all passengers' most sweet relief?

Oh Thou, whose glorious, yet contracted light,
Wrapt in night's mantle, stole into a manger;
Since my dark soul and brutish is Thy right,
To man of all beasts be not Thou a stranger:

Furnish and deck my soul, that Thou mayst have
A better lodging, than a rack, or grave.

George Herbert (1593-1633)

The Oxen

Christmas Eve, and twelve of the clock.
"Now they are all on their knees,"
An elder said as we sat in a flock
By the embers in hearthside ease.

We pictured the meek mild creatures where
They dwelt in their strawy pen,
Nor did it occur to one of us there
To doubt they were kneeling then.

So fair a fancy few would weave
In these years! Yet, I feel,
If someone said on Christmas Eve,
"Come; see the oxen kneel,

"In the lonely barton by yonder coomb
Our childhood used to know,"
I should go with him in the gloom,
Hoping it might be so.

Thomas Hardy (1840-1928)

The Christmas Life

'If you don't have a real tree, you don't bring
the Christmas life into the house.'
Josephine MacKinnon, aged 8

Bring in a tree, a young Norwegian spruce,
Bring hyacinths that rooted in the cold.
Bring winter jasmine as its buds unfold -
Bring the Christmas life into this house.

Bring red and green and gold, bring things that shine,
Bring candlesticks and music, food and wine.
Bring in your memories of Chistmas past.
Bring in your tears for all that you have lost.

Bring in the shepherd boy, the ox and ass,
Bring in the stillness of an icy night,
Bring in a birth, of hope and love and light.
Bring the Christmas life into this house.

Wendy Cope (1945-)

Abiding in the Fields. . .

To be ignorant is blessing, as a child is blessed
in its unknowing; better to yield to sun and wind,

to be stunned out of our wits – and to admit it –
by yowling storm and abrupt lightning, to be in awe

before the stars and their distinct music, to climb
into a tree to better look upon the earth; better to trust

to husbandry and offer out of poverty small gifts.
That night, one of the darkest, and brightest! sheep

shuffling and snuffling enough to bother us, yet all
I can remember is our stumbling over hump and lump

to touch upon the source. Sustenance proffered, out
of the rush of things that cause confusion, to some edge

where purpose might be glimpsed, and word shared. We left
poor gifts, feeling absolved of something, still unworthful.

John F. Deane (1943-)

Prosaic Interlude...

Extract from the index to
The Faber Book of Christmas by Simon Rae (1996)
as reported by Charles Boyle:

From *99 Interruptions*

71 I'm in a holding space. A woman is hanging red and silver balls on a plastic Christmas tree. Another woman comes out of a door, glances at me, looks at the cover of the file she is carrying, goes back into the room she came out of. A man comes out of another door, turns to lock it, tells me his colleague will be with me soon, heads off to lunch. A third woman comes out of another door and locks it behind her; she is clutching tissues to her face, she has a nosebleed; she unlocks the door the man came out of and goes in. The Christmas-tree woman is now arranging strands of tinsel around framed advertisements for mortgages and pensions. I ask her how much longer I will need to sit here and she looks at me as if that is a question no one in the history of the world has ever asked before. Together, we notice flecks of blood on the carpet. 'Festive,' she says.

Charles Boyle (1951-)

28

The Time Draws Near the Birth of Christ

The time draws near the birth of Christ:
>The moon is hid; the night is still;
>The Christmas bells from hill to hill
Answer each other in the mist.

Four voices of four hamlets round,
>From far and near, on mead and moor,
>Swell out and fail, as if a door
Were shut between me and the sound:

Each voice four changes on the wind,
>That now dilate, and now decrease,
>Peace and goodwill, goodwill and peace,
Peace and goodwill, to all mankind.

This year I slept and woke with pain,
>I almost wish'd no more to wake,
>And that my hold on life would break
Before I heard those bells again:

But they my troubled spirit rule,
>For they controll'd me when a boy;
>They bring me sorrow touch'd with joy,
The merry merry bells of Yule.

Alfred Tennyson (1809-1892)

A Neanderthal Meditation for Christmas

You used to hear them saying, *homo*
factus est, not *sapiens*, you notice,
as if, scooping the gene pool, he had caught up
all the long story prior to the day
our cousins first moved in next door.
We exchanged glances, we who had seen
the habitat grow up around us; we could guess
the skinny, noisy, tearful, combative,
twittering, twitching, homicidal neighbours
would be a headache. For one thing,
they never sat still long enough to hear
a sentence through, a sentence from
the long bone flutes inside
our hospitable nostrils, music
like waves' heaving to slow sonar pulses.
Their scratchy throats cackled one interruption
after another. And there was the rubbish
and dog poo thrown over the fence, and when
their children got to adolescence and discovered
alcohol and stuff, and music like pneumatic
drills all night, we really wondered.
It was as if they never could be sure
of where they were if they weren't
crying and quarrelling, as if someone had
left them in a great dark bombed-out cave,
a multi-storey car park or sports stadium, deserted,
no fire, no light, their catastrophic, flat,

colourless faces staring into the broken glass at night,
frightened that if they ever for a moment stopped
crying and quarrelling and interrupting, no-one
would find them. *Et homo*
factus, so that he walked into
the boiling kitchen where they all threw
knives and scalding water, and he stood
between them to save lives. But when
he spoke to them, what we could overhear
was like a distant echo of the bone flutes
and pitched waves we still caressed each other with,
quietly, behind locked doors, and we thought
something from what was scattered like the snow
back when we all began, the bright shards of mirror,
something had leapt the wall from the lost days
when we could sit and sing, out on the ragged lawn.
Sometimes we caught his eye over the wall.,
I could have sworn I saw him wink and heard him
sing under his breath, as if to say, This is our secret:
homo factus sum, not *sapiens* alone, you notice.

Rowan Williams (1950-)

Dover Beach

...

The Sea of Faith
Was once, too, at the full, and round earth's shore
Lay like the folds of a bright girdle furled.
But now I only hear
Its melancholy, long, withdrawing roar,
Retreating, to the breath
Of the night-wind, down the vast edges drear
And naked shingles of the world.

Ah, love, let us be true
To one another! for the world, which seems
To lie before us like a land of dreams,
So various, so beautiful, so new,
Hath really neither joy, nor love, nor light,
Nor certitude, nor peace, nor help for pain;
And we are here as on a darkling plain
Swept with confused alarms of struggle and flight,
Where ignorant armies clash by night.

Matthew Arnold (1822-1888)

The Rapper's Last Mass

Mark went Midnight Mass I stayed
Inside the inn where dwellers brayed
Lashed the din teeming poison
Stabbed at things they deemed annoying
But down below an earthy soup
Just swirled these careless prayers on loop

Claire went Midnight Mass I dithered
Persuaded to placate some spirits
Flicked the chin back deep hot plummet
Made fiery crimson of my stomach
But down the road the water sighed
To hear these rituals tested tired

Greg went Midnight Mass I slank
Away and flounced along the river
Chundered on its shingle flank
Then thought I heard a newborn whimper
And all around me moving air
Kept this newborn whimper there

A bobbing star now turns to listening
Seems to signal with its twinkling
But I just spit and lurch off thinking
How many more times can we kill him
Kill him kill him kill him

Charlie Dupré (1983-)

Watch Charlie Dupré performing 'The Rapper's
Last Mass' at:
https://www.youtube.com/watch?v=IwSSIVInE78

I Saw a Stable

I saw a stable, low and very bare,
A little child in a manger.
The Oxen knew him, had Him in their care,
To men he was a stranger.
The safety of the world was lying there,
And the world's danger.

Mary Elizabeth Coleridge (1861-1907)

Surya 4, 171

O People of the Scripture! Do not exaggerate in your religion not utter aught concerning Allah save the Truth. The Messiah, Jesus Son of Mary, was only a messenger of Allah, and His word which he conveyed unto Mary, and a spirit from Him. So believe in Allah and his messengers, and say not 'Three' – Cease! It is better for you! – Allah is only One God. Far is it removed from His transcendental majesty that he should have a son. His is all that is in the heavens and all that is in the earth. And Allah is sufficient as Defender.

Marmaduke Pickthall (1875-1936), from The Meaning of the Glorious Koran

The Innumerable Christ

'Other stars may have their Bethlehem,
and their Calvary too.'
(Professor J.Y. Simpson)

Wha kens on whatna Bethlehems
Earth twinkles like a star the nicht,
An' whatna shepherds lift their heids
In its unearthly licht?

'Yont a' the stars oor een can see
An' farther than their lichts can fly,
I' mony an unco warl' the nicht
The fatefu' bairnies cry.

I' mony an unco warl' the nicht
The lift gaes black as pitch at noon,
An' sideways on their chests the heids
O' endless Christs roll doon.

An' when the earth's as cauld's the mune
An' a' its folk are lang syne deid,
On coontless stars the Babe maun cry
An' the Crucified maun bleed.

Hugh MacDiarmid (1892-1978)

Ave Maria Gratia Plena

Was this His coming? I had hoped to see
A scene of wondrous glory, as was told
Of some great God who fell in a rain of gold
Broke open bars and fell on Danae:
Or a dread vision as when Semele,
Sickening for love and unappeased desire,
Prayed to see God's clear body, and the fire
Caught her brown limbs and slew her utterly.
With such glad dreams I sought this holy place,
And now with wondering eyes and heart I stand
Before this supreme mystery of Love:
Some kneeling girl with passionless pale face,
An angel with a lily in his hand,
And over both the white wings of a Dove.

Oscar Wilde (1854-1990)

A Slovak Christmas Tree

Above the altar floats the Christ Child;
Rosy, plump, baroque he floats free
From the round breasts of the Virgin Mary
Who is all, as they claim here, 'blood and milk'.
He floats in shimmering blue and gold
Beneath the branches of a gaunt tree.

Outside the church we wrap our natures
Against the cold wind and the snow.
Unleaved, linden, ash and beech show
The crookedness the Christ Child endures
From us; bare branches snow-blurred
That the cold wind creaks to and fro.

The Christ Child will burst his rosy bud
To the everlasting green of leaves,
But he'll be fruit for our unbelief
On a gaunt tree whose wood stains red
As each year our sins bud, leaf and shed
While we claim, disclaim, proclaim belief.

James Sutherland-Smith (1948-)

Christmas Holiday

Big-uddered piebald cattle low
The shivering chestnut stallion dozes
The fat wife sighs in her chair
Her lap is filled with paper roses
The poacher sleeps in the goose-girl's arms
Incurious after so much eating
All human beings are replete.

But the cock upon the dunghill feels
God's needle quiver in his brain
And thrice he crows: and at the sound
The sober and the tipsy men
Jump out of bed with one accord
And start the war again.

The fat wife comfortably sleeping
Sighs and licks her lips and smiles
But the goose-girl is weeping.

Alun Lewis (1915-1944)

Upon Christmas Eve

Vaile cobwebs from the white-ned floor
And let Arachne spin noe more;
With holly-bushes all adorned
Until the comeing of the more
And fancy then the Lord of Light is there
As he did once in Moses-bush appear

John Suckling (1609-1642)

Upon Christ His Birth

Strange News! a Cittie full? Will none give way
To lodge a guest that comes not every day?
Noe inne, nor tavern void? yet I descry
One empty place alone, where wee may ly:

In too much fullness is some want: but where?
Mens empty hearts: let's ask for lodging there.
But if they not admit us, then wee'le say
Their hearts, and as well as inn's, are made of clay.

John Suckling (1609-1642)

The Computer's First Christmas Card

```
jollymerry
hollyberry
jollyberry
merryholly
happyjolly
jollyjelly
jellybelly
bellymerry
hollyheppy
jollyMolly
marryJerry
merryHarry
hoppyBarry
heppyJarry
boppyheppy
berryjorry
jorryjolly
moppyjelly
Mollymerry
Jerryjolly
bellyboppy
jorryhoppy
hollymoppy
Barrymerry
Jarryhappy
happyboppy
boppyjolly
jollymerry
merrymerry
merrymerry
merryChris
ammerryasa
Chrismerrry
asMERRYCHR
YSANTHEMUM
```

Edwin Morgan (1920-2010)

The First Snow of Christmas

Snow makes a slight sound like a nurse's sleeve
And clings to the branches of the pine
Producing shapes like plaster casts
Round classical statues or broken limbs;
This one a satyr shiftingly obscene,
That one an arm set at right angles.

Beneath our windows a family searches
For a lost puppy or a kitten.
They shine thin torch beams on the snow
And I'm reminded of sunlight
Wavering across the seabed in patches
Until a shadow falls across the glitter.

It's not a cloud across the moon but the gypsy
We sent packing earlier today.
I'd given him money three days before,
Complimented the ink-blue suit
He'd received at the pastor's door.
He was bald, single-toothed and skinny,

An unshaven Nosferatu though not ashen
And afraid of light, but mahogany.
In one hand he carried a violin.
His other gripped my own, his thumbnail
Digging to leave a wedge shaped flaw
That still aches as the winter cold sets in.

I rub it as he pauses in the snow
And takes his violin from its case
To play a scratchy, hardwood music.
He salutes our windows then hides his face
As the torches are clicked off one by one
And a rough northerly begins to blow.

James Sutherland-Smith (1948-)

The Second Coming

Turning and turning in the widening gyre
The falcon cannot hear the falconer;
Things fall apart; the centre cannot hold;
Mere anarchy is loosed upon the world,
The blood-dimmed tide is loosed, and everywhere
The ceremony of innocence is drowned;
The best lack all conviction, while the worst
Are full of passionate intensity.

Surely some revelation is at hand;
Surely the Second Coming is at hand.
The Second Coming! Hardly are those words out
When a vast image out of Spiritus Mundi
Troubles my sight: somewhere in sands of the desert
A shape with lion body and the head of a man,
A gaze blank and pitiless as the sun,
Is moving its slow thighs, while all about it
Reel shadows of the indignant desert birds.
The darkness drops again; but now I know
That twenty centuries of stony sleep
Were vexed to nightmare by a rocking cradle,
And what rough beast, its hour come round at last,
Slouches towards Bethlehem to be born?

W.B Yeats (1885-1939)

Damp after Christmas

and us on the bench with a downhill view
of the back of our house, the running curve
of the street, us with a view of windows,
the windows we stand behind, tracking
the passage of prams, of people with tools
for allotments, the blurred limbs of dogs,

us on a bench with a downhill view
of the running curve of the street,
of stone long mortared into homes —
clotting the dip and rise of fields,
built by men who made four square,
set lavatories up garden paths,

homes where David and Mrs McPhee
will vanish into names, words we pause
before speaking aloud, *can't imagine*
the loss, really sorry for —
homes where children are seeded
under blankets, urged into view

Jenny Hockey (1946-)

Nativity

Immensity cloistered in thy dear womb,
Now leaves His well-belov'd imprisonment,
There He hath made Himself to His intent
Weak enough, now into the world to come;
But O, for thee, for Him, hath the inn no room?
Yet lay Him in this stall, and from the Orient,
Stars and wise men will travel to prevent
The effect of Herod's jealous general doom.
Seest thou, my soul, with thy faith's eyes, how He
Which fills all place, yet none holds Him, doth lie?
Was not His pity towards thee wondrous high,
That would have need to be pitied by thee?
Kiss Him, and with Him into Egypt go,
With His kind mother, who partakes thy woe.

John Donne (1572-1631)

A Hymn on the Nativity of My Saviour

I sing the birth was born tonight,
The Author both of life and light;
　　The angels so did sound it,
And like the ravished shepherds said,
Who saw the light, and were afraid,
　　Yet searched, and true they found it.

The Son of God, the eternal King,
That did us all salvation bring,
　　And freed the soul from danger;
He whom the whole world could not take,
The Word, which heaven and earth did make,
　　Was now laid in a manger.

The Father's wisdom willed it so,
The Son's obedience knew no "No,"
　　Both wills were in one stature;
And as that wisdom had decreed,
The Word was now made Flesh indeed,
　　And took on Him our nature.

What comfort by Him do we win?
Who made Himself the Prince of sin,
　　To make us heirs of glory?
To see this Babe, all innocence,
A Martyr born in our defense,
　　Can man forget this storie?

Ben Jonson (1572-1637)

Four Calling Birds

chosen by Martyn Crucefix

i / Mother and Child

'I syng of a mayden'

I syng of a mayden
that is matcheles,
king of alle kinges
to her sone she chees.

He cam also stille
there his moder was
as dew in Aprylle,
that fallyt on the gras.

He cam also stille
to his modres bowr
as dew in Aprylle,
that falleth on the flowr.

He cam also stille
there his moder lay
as dew in Aprylle,
that falleth on the spray.

Moder and mayden
was nevere noon but she:
well may swich a lady
Godes moder be.

Trad. 15th century

50

The Heart-in-Waiting

Jesus walked through whispering wood:
'I am pale blossom, I am blood berry,
I am rough bark, I am sharp thorn.
This is the place where you will be born.'

Jesus went down to the skirl of the sea:
'I am long reach, I am fierce comber,
I am keen saltspray, I am spring tide.'
He pushed the cup of the sea aside

And heard the sky which breathed-and-blew:
'I am the firmament, I am shape-changer,
I cradle and carry and kiss and roar,
I am infinite roof and floor.'

All day he walked, he walked all night,
Then Jesus came to the heart at dawn.
'Here and now,' said the heart-in-waiting,
'This is the place where you must be born.'

Kevin Crossley-Holland

Hymn for Christmas Day

The Shepherds watch their flocks by night,
Beneath the moon's unclouded light,
All around is calm and still,
Save the murm'ring of the rill:
When lo! a form of light appears,
And on the awe-struck Shepherds' ears
Are words, of peace and comfort flowing
From lips with love celestial glowing.
Spiritual forms are breaking
Through the gloom, their voices taking
Part in the adoring song
Of the bright angelic throng.
Wondering, the Shepherds bend
Their steps to Bethlehem and wend
To a poor and crowded inn: –
Tremblingly their way they win
To the stable, where they find
The Redeemer of mankind,
Just born into this world of danger,
Lying in an humble manger.
And they spread abroad each word
Which that joyful night they'd heard,
And they glorified the name
Of their gracious God, Who came
Himself to save from endless woe
The offspring of this world below.

Christina Rossetti

St Ita's Lullaby

Hush my sweet Jesus, hush my little lamb
Lamps are being lit in Killeedy
Footsteps are failing, the sun sinking down.

Hush my sweet Jesus, hush my little lamb
Streams hug their beds near Killeedy
The straw in the barns is fragrant and warm.

Hush my sweet Jesus, hush my little lamb
The wind falls asleep in Killeedy
The moon's dissolving and the night is calm.

Hush my sweet Jesus, hush my little lamb
Angels descend on Killeedy
A snowfall of stars until the new dawn.

Hush my sweet Jesus, hush my little lamb
Hush, hush, hush . . .

James Harpur

Upon Christ's Nativity

From three dark places Christ came forth this day;
From first his Father's bosom, where he lay
Concealed till now; then from the typic law,
Where we his manhood but by figures saw;
And lastly from his mother's womb he came
To us, a perfect God and perfect Man.
   Now in a manger lies the eternal Word:
The Word he is, yet can no speech afford;
He is the Bread of Life, yet hungry lies;
The Living Fountain, yet for drink He cries;
He cannot help or clothe himself at need
Who did the lilies clothe and ravens feed;
He is the Light of Lights, yet now doth shroud
His glory with our nature as a cloud.
He came to us a little one, that we
Like little children might in malice be;
Little he is, and wrapped in clouts, lest he
Might strike us dead if clothed with majesty.
   Christ had four beds and those not soft, nor brave:
The Virgin's womb, the manger, cross, and grave.
The angels sing this day, and so will I
That have more reason to be glad than they.

Rowland Watkyns

54

The adoration of the kings
after Pieter Breugel the Elder

Everything looks rough-hewn and doltish
and has done since my eyes
began to betray me now unreliably I peer
through thick blue saucers of glass

yet I feel how these strangers stir us—
this one with the pinched face of a carpenter
more than a king though the bold red
of his sleeves and collar and the aureate bowl

his fingers dandle appear to be rich indeed
and wholly out of place in our stable yard
where we find this squalling child
reluctant and bollock-naked as far as I can see

then this older one with his lank grey hair
stooping as if to show off his ermine trim
and his extraordinarily long pink sleeves
(I see them more clearly than anything else)

he positions his hat and mace in the dirt
to offer something I can't make out
beside me the black skin and sharp leather smell
of the third who proffers an elaborate gift

of green and yellow—it must be gold and jade
yet smells sweetly of spices to me
a sort of sweetness like nothing I've known
and I can tell you I'm good with odours

even better with my ears which are sharp enough
to trace the munching commentary
of the ass in the byre the shifting of the crowd
and the hiss of doltish Piet with his lips

to the poor father's ear telling him I suppose
what we all know of the difference
in their ages and of the ominous signs
from the fractious boy even the fact the child

cannot possibly be his—shit-for-brains Piet
in his green snood has never been one to look
beyond the obvious not one to let gossip
go abegging yet the young mother's face has

turned now half-obscured as if she wants us
to believe there's something in all this
not the sighted nor the blind can fathom
some secret she and her strangers are keeping

Martyn Crucefix

The Mother of God

The threefold terror of love; a fallen flare
Through the hollow of an ear;
Wings beating about the room;
The terror of all terrors that I bore
The Heavens in my womb.

Had I not found content among the shows
Every common woman knows,
Chimney corner, garden walk,
Or rocky cistern where we tread the clothes
And gather all the talk?

What is this flesh I purchased with my pains,
This fallen star my milk sustains,
This love that makes my heart's blood stop
Or strikes a Sudden chill into my bones
And bids my hair stand up?

W. B. Yeats

God is Born

The history of the cosmos
is the history of the struggle of becoming.
When the dim flux of unformed life
struggled, convulsed back and forth upon itself,
and broke at last into light and dark
came into existence as light,
came into existence as cold shadow
then every atom of the cosmos trembled with delight.
Behold, God is born!
He is bright light!
He is pitch dark and cold!

And in the great struggle of intangible chaos
when, at a certain point, a drop of water
  began to drip downwards
and a breath of vapour began to wreathe up
Lo again the shudder of bliss through all the atoms!
Oh, God is born!
Behold, he is born wet!
Look, he hath movement upward! He spirals!

And so, in the great aeons of accomplishment and debacle
from time to time the wild crying of every electron:
Lo! God is born!

D. H. Lawrence

A Child of the Snows

There is heard a hymn when the panes are dim,
And never before or again,
When the nights are strong with a darkness long,
And the dark is alive with rain.

Never we know but in sleet and in snow,
The place where the great fires are,
That the midst of the earth is a raging mirth
And the heart of the earth a star.

And at night we win to the ancient inn
Where the child in the frost is furled,
We follow the feet where all souls meet
At the inn at the end of the world.

The gods lie dead where the leaves lie red,
For the flame of the sun is flown,
The gods lie cold where the leaves lie gold,
And a child comes forth alone.

G. K. Chesterton

ii / Hearth and Home

Chris'mas Invitation

Come down to-morrow night; an' mind,
Don't leave thy fiddle-bag behind;
We'll sheake a lag, an' drink a cup
O'eale, to keep wold Chris'mas up.

An' let thy sister teake thy earm,
The walk won't do her any harm;
There's noo dirt now to spweil her frock,
The ground's a-vroze so hard's a rock.

You won't meet any stranger's feace,
But only naighbours o'the pleace,
An' Stowe, an' Combe; an' two or dree
Vrom uncle's up at Rookery.

An' thou wu'lt vind a rwosy feace,
An' peair ov eyes so black as sloos,
The prettiest woones in all the pleace, –
I'm sure I needen tell thee whose.

We got a back-bran', dree girt logs
So much as dree ov us can car;
We'll put 'em up athirt the dogs,
An meake a vier to the bar.

An' ev'ry woone shall tell his teale,
An' ev'ry woone shall zing his zong,
An' ev'ry woone wull drink his eale
To love an' frien'ship all night long.

We'll snap the tongs, we'll have a ball,
We'll sheake the house, we'll lift the ruf,
We'll romp an' meake the maidens squall,
A' catchen o'm at blind-man's buff.

Zoo come to-morrow night; an' mind,
Don't leave thy fiddle-bag behind;
We'll sheake a lag, an' drink a cup
O'eale, to keep wold Chris'mas up.

William Barnes

The House of Hospitalities

Here we broached the Christmas barrel,
    Pushed up the charred log-ends;
Here we sang the Christmas carol,
    And called in friends.

Time has tired me since we met here
    When the folk now dead were young,
Since the viands were outset here
    And quaint songs sung.

And the worm has bored the viol
    That used to lead the tune,
Rust eaten out the dial
    That struck night's noon.

Now no Christmas brings in neighbours,
    And the New Year comes unlit;
Where we sang the mole now labours,
    And spiders knit.

Yet at midnight if here walking,
    When the moon sheets wall and tree,
I see forms of old time talking,
    Who smile on me.

Thomas Hardy

Christmas 2020

Obeying lockdown rules,
all of us were at home.

So our neighbours at number 3
organised a carol concert.

Dressed up in Santa hats
with tails and tinkling bells,

they parked their music stands,
in the middle of the road.

The stands were dressed in tinsel
and winking coloured lights.

Tom played the violin,
his brother played the sax,

and we sang from the windows
into the lamplit dark.

Joan Michelson

The True Christmas

So stick up ivy and the bays,
And then restore the heathen ways.
Green will remind you of the spring,
Though this great day denies the thing.
And mortifies the earth and all
But your wild revels, and loose hall.
Could you wear flowers, and roses strow
Blushing upon your breasts' warm snow,
That very dress your lightness will
Rebuke, and wither at the ill.
The brightness of this day we owe
Not unto music, masque, nor show:
Nor gallant furniture, nor plate;
But to the manger's mean estate.
His life while here, as well as birth,
Was but a check to pomp and mirth;
And all man's greatness you may see
Condemned by his humility.
    Then leave your open house and noise,
To welcome him with holy joys,
And the poor shepherd's watchfulness:
Whom light and hymns from Heaven did bless.
What you abound with, cast abroad
To those that want, and ease your load.
Who empties thus, will bring more in;
But riot is both loss and sin.
Dress finely what comes not in sight,
And then you keep your Christmas right.

Henry Vaughan

Her Dream at Christmas

She returned to church after years
(not penitent, rather curious
about how things had altered there)
but she wasn't prepared for this.

In place of the old-style communion,
where thin priests would grimly spare
a dry biscuit, and a sniff of wine
was all the drink they'd ever share...

instead of that, she saw this:
there was nut-loaf on the choir stall,
with each prayer book a banana-split.
There was quiche, crab salad, lemon fool.

There on the font sat a turkey roast,
parsnips, carrots, sprouts spilled over.
The whole church was a perfect feast!
On the pews stood raspberry pavlova.

And where the faithful knelt in line
drinks were unsteadily dispensed
from a box of chilled Italian wine.
She knew the price must be immense.

She fled back home and found a place
of hunger – rooms of emptiness.
Then she fell asleep for forty days
and woke with this need to confess.

Martyn Crucefix

That's the Art Deco Odeon
on London's Holloway Road

In a home of Mum's novels, Dad's only book
was a creased copy of *The Autobiography*

of Malcolm X. I held it in the Black
of my palm the dawn Dad died, its heft

growing. I watched Spike Lee's biopic, *Malcolm X*
with Dad. The Odeon's* screen is still glowing

on rows of Afro hairdos – the film's magic
connected us, in our minds dismantling

stereotypes Hollywood helped build for us.
It was like watching Lenny Henry at Christmas –

his character, Deakus, sipping Guinness
like men who played dominoes at my auntie's parties.

Post Lego and Christmas rice and peas, there was Lenny
and our laughter, Dad's laughter, Dad's laughter…

Marvin Thompson

The Reminder

While I watch the Christmas blaze
Paint the room with ruddy rays,
Something makes my vision glide
To the frosty scene outside.

There, to reach a rotting berry,
Toils a thrush, - constrained to very
Dregs of food by sharp distress,
Taking such with thankfulness.

Why, O starving bird, when I
One day's joy would justify,
And put misery out of view,
Do you make me notice you!

Thomas Hardy

Mum's Garden, December

Okay to the thirteen green parakeets
on the bare apple tree,
noisily celebrating their ancestral break-out
from Kew Gardens.

Okay to the woodpecker
with red cockade
feasting on lawn grubs
for over an hour.

Thumbs-up to the usual suspects,
thrushes, magpies,
crows, reservoir-seagulls.
But, natural world, you have to be kidding...

On the garden's tall fir tree,
one ungainly fairy
tops the green Christmas tree,
hunch-perched heron

surveying the edibility scene
(no garden hereabouts
without its goldfish pond).

Contemptuous
of crows ganging up to rasp
No Herons Allowed!

he takes his lofty time before launching
his foldable legs and greybeard wings
into the breakfast-time sky.

Who'd think this treetop gawk
had ballet-work in him,
our light-fantastic visitant?

Penelope Shuttle

Hard Walk

21ˢᵗ December. The map whose one task was to guide me to Marble Hill led me instead to the park. When searching for a seat, a thought came, went and came to my head again, and I strolled on to the next bench, as the first one was taken by a child who refused to stand up for her older sister but lay down under the bench until the mother picked her up from the ground. *Keep on walking* said the thought. The thought was not mine. My sister told me she wanted me to carry on walking as I had been house-bound for a month. I was unsure where to turn next as the House Café was closed. I forgot about visiting the grotto, but remembered that my sister was alone at home, and I was alone in Ice House Quarter, and by now, light was growing as the sky cleared, and shadows of a holm oak tree were stretching across a small door of the icehouse mound. I stopped walking. It was here the child from Ice House Quarter ran to me and skipped around me in circles.

You bring bad luck, my mother said as she watched me walking around her in circles. I suppose this was where children walked in circles around women, bonded with mothers and sisters by playing games. Light-headedness came to me as I strolled in circles through the park. Beyond Marble Hill House, another brief garden of docks and suchlike weeds and, as my mind was still, I picked some of them. My stroll began like any other stroll, alone and peaceful. This time I could not forget past walks through sites of English Heritage. Before I was a hiker, I wrote about strolling and rambling. An imagined hill, rivers and pathways brought me here and I paused at the entrance long enough for me to see the grounds of the house.

chamber of ivy
smell of the pine   barren stone
a cave behind bars

Denise Saul

The House of Christmas

There fared a mother driven forth
Out of an inn to roam;
In the place where she was homeless
All men are at home.
The crazy stable close at hand,
With shaking timber and shifting sand,
Grew a stronger thing to abide and stand
Than the square stones of Rome.

For men are homesick in their homes,
And strangers under the sun,
And they lay their heads in a foreign land
Whenever the day is done.
Here we have battle and blazing eyes,
And chance and honour and high surprise,
But our homes are under miraculous skies
Where the yule tale was begun.

A Child in a foul stable,
Where the beasts feed and foam;
Only where He was homeless
Are you and I at home;
We have hands that fashion and heads that know,
But our hearts we lost - how long ago!
In a place no chart nor ship can show
Under the sky's dome.

This world is wild as an old wives' tale,
And strange the plain things are,
The earth is enough and the air is enough
For our wonder and our war;
But our rest is as far as the fire-drake swings

And our peace is put in impossible things
Where clashed and thundered unthinkable wings
Round an incredible star.

To an open house in the evening
Home shall men come,
To an older place than Eden
And a taller town than Rome.
To the end of the way of the wandering star,
To the things that cannot be and that are,
To the place where God was homeless
And all men are at home.

G. K. Chesterton

iii / Far and Near

The Gypsy

A fortnight before Christmas Gypsies were everywhere:
Vans were drawn up on wastes, women trailed to the fair.
'My gentleman,' said one, 'You've got a lucky face.'
'And you've a luckier,' I thought, 'if such a grace
And impudence in rags are lucky.' 'Give a penny
For the poor baby's sake.' 'Indeed I have not any
Unless you can give change for a sovereign, my dear.'
'Then just half a pipeful of tobacco can you spare?'
I gave it. With that much victory she laughed content.
I should have given more, but off and away she went
With her baby and her pink sham flowers to rejoin
The rest before I could translate to its proper coin
Gratitude for her grace. And I paid nothing then,
As I pay nothing now with the dipping of my pen
For her brother's music when he drummed the tambourine
And stamped his feet, which made the workmen passing grin,
While his mouth-organ changed to a rascally Bacchanal dance
'Over the hills and far away'. This and his glance
Outlasted all the fair, farmer and auctioneer,
Cheap-jack, balloon-man, drover with crooked stick, and steer,
Pig, turkey, goose, and duck, Christmas corpses to be.
Not even the kneeling ox had eyes like the Romany.
That night he peopled for me the hollow wooded land,
More dark and wild than stormiest heavens,
                                        that I searched and scanned
Like a ghost new-arrived. The gradations of the dark
Were like an underworld of death, but for the spark
In the Gypsy boy's black eyes as he played and stamped his tune,
'Over the hills and far away', and a crescent moon.

Edward Thomas

Cento

All the trees that are in the wood
are wrapped in swathing bands
heat is in the very sod
and thorns infest the ground

Snow has fallen, snow on snow
mountains in reply
sing gloria in excelsis deo
silent ships go by

Fast away the old year passes
Christmas comes once more
dressed in gay apparel lasses
beg from door to door

Poor boys shelter by the fence
gathering winter fuel
heedless of the wind's lament
the holly decks the hall

Brightly shines the morning star
by prophet bards foretold
after the running of the deer
shall come the age of gold

Night will break and glory shake
the rising of the sun
the old familiar carols play
pa rum pum pum pum

Kate Bingham

Christmas Cards

Slip through the letter box with messages:
Some bland, some more intense, some aching with
Bereavements, wives abandoned, loss of jobs.

The annual contact on a patient card.
'See you next year' some say and quite forget
Before the ink is dry. A plaster patch

That leaves no sticky mark on minor wounds
However much the cover faces please
With coloured art or kitsch or nearly art.

One threatens every time in wiry script
'This is the last card I shall send. I am
Too old now'. Still it slides into my hand.

And there is one that comes anonymous,
Unsigned, the postmark adds its mystery,
A smudge, a ghost behind this paper mask?

Perhaps there'll be a few to tuck away
After the show, in an old envelope,
Fingered at times because the sender once

Carved hope into a fraction of your years;
Or others will imply 'I am still here' –
A comma on your page a life ago.

Lotte Kramer

Moonless darkness stands between

Moonless darkness stands between.
Past, the Past, no more be seen!
But the Bethlehem-star may lead me
To the sight of Him Who freed me
From the self that I have been.
Make me pure, Lord: Thou art holy;
Make me meek, Lord: Thou wert lowly;
Now beginning, and alway:
Now begin, on Christmas day.

Gerard Manley Hopkins

Enter the theologians

The wild, unsettled sound of
these thin, in-between days –

there is no switch to throw the
line back, just a cut, a cut,

a cut again, until the edge
of what you can see starts

to break down. Enter the theologians,
telling you: in these fuzzy

moments is where you discover
the space to dispute, to revel,

to reveal, to party play love,
to link yourself to the best

of yourself, to bask in a band
of a glory you deserve.

Rishi Dastidar

Christmas at Sea

The sheets were frozen hard, and they cut the naked hand;
The decks were like a slide, where a seaman scarce could stand;
The wind was a nor'wester, blowing squally off the sea;
And cliffs and spouting breakers were the only things a-lee....

We gave the South a wider berth, for there the tide-race roared;
But every tack we made we brought the North Head close aboard:
So's we saw the cliffs and houses, and the breakers running high,
And the coastguard in his garden, with his glass against his eye.

The frost was on the village roofs as white as ocean foam;
The good red fires were burning bright in every 'long-shore home;
The windows sparkled clear, and the chimneys volleyed out;
And I vow we sniffed the victuals as the vessel went about.

The bells upon the church were rung with a mighty jovial cheer;
For it's just that I should tell you how (of all days in the year)
This day of our adversity was blessed Christmas morn,
And the house above the coastguard's was the house where I was
born....

And well I knew the talk they had, the talk that was of me,
Of the shadow on the household and the son that went to sea;
And O the wicked fool I seemed, in every kind of way,
To be here and hauling frozen ropes on blessed Christmas Day....

She staggered to her bearings, but the sails were new and good,
And the ship smelt up to windward just as though she understood.
As the winter's day was ending, in the entry of the night,
We cleared the weary headland and passed below the light.

And they heaved a mighty breath, every soul on board but me,
As they saw her nose again pointing handsome out to sea;
But all that I could think of, in the darkness and the cold,
Was just that I was leaving home and my folks were growing old.

Robert Louis Stevenson

Not the new poetry
A blackbird pecking
an apple left hanging
on the tree – a red apple
with a white cap of snow.

It's like nothing in the world
but another blackbird
landing on another branch
which quivers, shedding
a little snow.

Owls calling on a winter night
which to the listener
sleepless in his bed
sounds like 'Where, where?'
and an answering 'Here, here'.

But who knows, who knows,
silence returning
with a fever of human fears

Snow like thought
because it arrives
seemingly from nowhere
small flakes wandering
sideways
down & up & down

then faster, heavier
bringing up
deeper silence
from some place one dreamed of
that was always there.

Jeremy Hooker

The Mystic's Christmas

'All hail!' the bells of Christmas rang,
'All hail!' the monks at Christmas sang,
The merry monks who kept with cheer
The gladdest day of all their year.

But still apart, unmoved thereat,
A pious elder brother sat
Silent, in his accustomed place,
With God's sweet peace upon his face.

'Why sitt'st thou thus?' his brethren cried,
'It is the blessed Christmas-tide;
The Christmas lights are all aglow,
The sacred lilies bud and blow....

'Rejoice with us; no more rebuke
Our gladness with thy quiet look.'
The gray monk answered, 'Keep, I pray,
Even as ye list, the Lord's birthday

'Let heathen Yule fires flicker red
Where thronged refectory feasts are spread;
With mystery-play and masque and mime
And wait-songs speed the holy time!

'They needs must grope who cannot see,
The blade before the ear must be;
As ye are feeling I have felt,
And where ye dwell I too have dwelt.
'But now, beyond the things of sense,

Beyond occasions and events,
I know, through God's exceeding grace,
Release from form and time and space.

'I listen, from no mortal tongue,
To hear the song the angels sung;
And wait within myself to know
The Christmas lilies bud and blow...

John Greenleaf Whittier

iv / Light and Sound

The Minstrels Played

The minstrels played their Christmas tune
To-night beneath my cottage-eaves;
While, smitten by a lofty moon,
The encircling laurels, thick with leaves,
Gave back a rich and dazzling sheen,
That overpowered their natural green.

Through hill and valley every breeze
Had sunk to rest with folded wings:
Keen was the air, but could not freeze,
Nor check, the music of the strings;
So stout and hardy were the band
That scraped the chords with strenuous hand.

And who but listened? – till was paid
Respect to every inmate's claim:
The greeting given, the music played,
In honour of each household name,
Duly pronounced with lusty call,
And 'Merry Christmas' wished to all.

William Wordsworth

Thursday, Christmas Eve, 1874

Writing Christmas letters all the morning. In the afternoon I went to the Church with Dora and Teddy to put up the Christmas decorations. Dora has been very busy for some days past making the straw letters for the Christmas text. Fair Rosamund and good Elizabeth Knight came to the Church to help us and worked heartily and well. They had made some pretty ivy knots and bunches for the pulpit panels and the ivy blossoms cleverly whitened with flour looked just like white flowers.

The churchwarden Jacob Knight was sitting by his sister in front of the roaring fire. We were talking of the death of Major Torrens on the ice at Corsham pond yesterday. Speaking of people slipping and falling on ice the good churchwarden sagely remarked, 'Some do fall on their faces and some do fall on their rumps. And they as do hold their selves uncommon stiff do most in generally fall on their rumps.'

I took old John Bryant a Christmas packet of tea and sugar and raisins from my Mother. The old man had covered himself almost entirely over in his bed to keep himself warm, like a marmot in its nest. He said, 'If I live till New Year's Day I shall have seen ninety-six New Years.' He said also, I do often see things flying about me, thousands and thousands of them about half the size of a large pea, and they are red, white, blue and yellow and all colours. I asked Mr. Morgan what they were and he said they were the spirits of just men made perfect.'

Francis Kilvert

The Circuit

Once more out of the shoe-box
(Christmas Accessories) dear tangled friends
With your plaited emerald flex
And familiar chime of chip-chink
Tumbling over my wrist, for the mind's
Ease for a moment I have you to thank

For my father's warm hand resting
Briefly on mine as again together
We number the dead ones and the wrong
Connections, restoring a light
Whose fitful flick and quiver
Is the love we shall celebrate

Tomorrow with the decked tree
Earthed in its yearly circuit
Of recurrence. When I say
Happy Christmas my own ghost
Will shine along the branches, lit
By all that is never lost

Though very soon forgotten. In two weeks
We shall be back here, dulled
And searching for this battered box I take
You from tonight to be, dear tangled friends,
A light of the world
Before the dark descends.

John Mole

December

Thou day of happy sound and mirth,
That long wi' childish memory stays,
How blessed around the cottage hearth
I met thee in my boyish days,
Harping wi' rapture's dreaming joys
O'er presents that thy coming found,
The welcome sight of little toys,
The Christmas gifts of comers-round:

'The wooden horse wi' arching head
Drawn upon wheels around the room,
The gilded coach of ginger bread
And many-coloured sugar plumb;
Gilt-covered books for pictures sought
Or stories childhood loves to tell,
Wi' many an urgent promise bought
To get tomorrows lesson well;

And many a thing a minute's sport
Left broken on the sanded floor
When we would leave our play and court
Our parents' promises for more,
Tho' manhood bids such raptures die
And throws such toys away as vain,
Yet memory loves to turn her eye
And talk such pleasures o'er again

Around the glowing hearth at night
The harmless laugh and Winter tale
Goes round – while parting friends delight
To toast each other o'er their ale.
The cotter oft wi' quiet zeal
Will musing o'er his Bible lean
While in the dark the lovers steal
To kiss and toy behind the screen.

John Clare

Christmas Eve

A stone replacement in her ring
and collected on Christmas Eve

but even as we prepare to watch
Carols from King's, the ring

has lost another (or the same)
stone. The carpet is awash

with glitter, with litter from
presents. What chance of finding

a small fallen star of
green as the choristers sing

from their everlasting fenlight
to a deep and dreamless sleep?

John Greening

Lights

I like to stay in and watch. Often I wake in the night to a static silence, a slow muffled note and I know they'll be there when I go to the window / dancing, or I'm sitting with a glass of milk as snow falls outside, a long time after I've come in from the snow, sometimes milk or sometimes / whisky, I feel their uneasy moves before I see them. They know I'm watching. They are dancing / for me. Lefteris is different. He likes to drive out of town / always believes things will be better elsewhere, after all that's why he's here, believes we will be closer to them on the other side of the mountain. // One time he took Asta's car and he's calling for me under my window, I put my glass down and hurry on with my boots again, don't even button my coat / we drive along the fjord through the tunnel in the rock out to the deserted valley on the other side with the long name no one remembers and where the road drops off the cliff into darkness he stops / just in time. A bird stirs against the stone ledge as we lie back on the ticking bonnet looking upwards and waiting and waiting and I want to go back home to my glass of milk and my bed / but some people just want to lose themselves in beauty, as if beauty can't exist until you have burnt up in it. / On the drive home Lefteris switches off the headlights he sees the stars and not the road. //

Nancy Campbell

A Winter Morning

Even with that east wind and the snow
Excluded, it was ghostly cold
Walking through the woods this morning;
Each branch as velvet as a young deer's
Horn, the hoar frost had so textured them;
Dry leaves, veined and brittle,
Crackled underfoot, and one little
Brown bird, constantly ahead of me,
Was looking for something.

Neil Curry

Noel: Christmas Eve 1913

Pax hominibus bonae voluntatis

A frosty Christmas Eve
  when the stars were shining
Fared I forth alone
  where westward falls the hill,
And from many a village
  in the water'd valley
Distant music reach'd me
  peals of bells aringing:
The constellated sounds
  ran sprinkling on earth's floor
As the dark vault above
  with stars was spangled o'er.

Then sped my thoughts to keep
  that first Christmas of all
When the shepherds watching
  by their folds ere the dawn
Heard music in the fields
  and marvelling could not tell
Whether it were angels
  or the bright stars singing.

Now blessed be the tow'rs
  that crown England so fair
That stand up strong in prayer
  unto God for our souls
Blessed be their founders
  (said I) an' our country folk
Who are ringing for Christ
  in the belfries to-night
With arms lifted to clutch

the rattling ropes that race
Into the dark above
    and the mad romping din.

But to me heard afar
    it was starry music
Angels' song, comforting
    as the comfort of Christ
When he spake tenderly
    to his sorrowful flock:
The old words came to me
    by the riches of time
Mellow'd and transfigured
    as I stood on the hill
Heark'ning in the aspect
    of th' eternal silence.

Robert Bridges

Supply

More through a faint vibration of the air
on our skin than by the ear,
we feel his arrival and hurry out –
leave the unfamiliar house for a darkness that
to our urban eyes is solid pitch,
nothing close, no middle, no sense of distance,
just a freezing rural December night
and whatever we can feel beneath our feet.
And there he is, rear wheels slipping in the mud
frictionless as any proper god –
come with the intent of supplying us
with food and drink through the winter solstice.
Rotund, in the spill of his van's light,
a pair of plump hands on hips, legs apart,
he stands there laughing at his predicament,
then punches away at the faint
signal on his phone but the place is too remote.
We offer to help him out –
begin to stumble to and fro in the lane,
in his rear-lights each like a crimson-faced clown –
trying gravel shovelled from the farm drive,
trying terracotta roof tiles
someone has tipped beside the bramble hedge.
We search for anything we might wedge
in the black slithering mess under his tyres,
straw, cardboard, logs, ironic prayers.
But the van still snarls like a tethered beast
and rocks to and fro like a helpless
child that fights the confines of its cradle . . .
Then he dismisses us with a smile.
He sends us back to light and warmth,
saying something like *it's what I'm here for.*

We shut the door, relieved, to be honest.
We leave him to the closing vice of frost
and next morning scarves of mist
replace the dark that with him have vanished.
Wheel ruts, gravel, red tiles broken:
we laugh in daylight – did this really happen?
Outside, there is little evidence to show.
Inside, shelves overflow.

Martyn Crucefix

'Ring out, wild bells'

Ring out, wild bells, to the wild sky,
  The flying cloud, the frosty light:
  The year is dying in the night;
Ring out, wild bells, and let him die.

Ring out the old, ring in the new,
  Ring, happy bells, across the snow:
  The year is going, let him go;
Ring out the false, ring in the true.

Ring out the grief that saps the mind
  For those that here we see no more;
  Ring out the feud of rich and poor,
Ring in redress to all mankind.

Ring out a slowly dying cause,
  And ancient forms of party strife;
  Ring in the nobler modes of life,
With sweeter manners, purer laws.

Ring out the want, the care, the sin,
  The faithless coldness of the times;
  Ring out, ring out my mournful rhymes
But ring the fuller minstrel in.

Ring out false pride in place and blood,
  The civic slander and the spite;
  Ring in the love of truth and right,
Ring in the common love of good.

Ring out old shapes of foul disease;
  Ring out the narrowing lust of gold;

Ring out the thousand wars of old,
Ring in the thousand years of peace.

Ring in the valiant man and free,
    The larger heart, the kindlier hand;
    Ring out the darkness of the land,
Ring in the Christ that is to be.

Alfred Tennyson

Envoi

Yule's come, and Yule's gane,
And we hae feasted weel,
Sae Jock maun to his flail again,
And Jenny to her wheel.

Trad.

Acknowledgments

My portion of this book could not have been compiled without the unstinting generosity of my friend John Birtwhistle, who shared his research with me. Thanks also to *The Tablet* and two of its editors – Catherine Pepinster and Brendan Walsh – who commissioned two features for their Christmas issues of 2015 and 2019, in which many of these poems were first published together. Thanks also to Carcanet Press, for giving permission to re-publish poems by Edwin Morgan and Hugh MacDiarmid, and to Faber & Faber and its author, Wendy Cope, for giving us permission to reprint 'The Christmas Life', which first appeared in *Christmas Poems* (2017). And also to the poets who have generously allowed me to print their poems or translations here: Alison Brackenbury, Charles Boyle, Hilary Davies, Charlie Dupré, James Sutherland-Smith, John F. Deane, Jenny Hockey and Rowan Williams. An especial expression of gratitude also goes to Papillote Press of London and Roseau, Dominica for permission to print a poem by Phyllis Shand Allfrey. The two poems by James Sutherland-Smith were first published in *Popeye in Belgrade* (Carcanet, 2008).

Michael Glover

I am very grateful to Michael Glover for inviting me to collaborate on compiling this anthology. What a pleasure it has been to read, research, invite and select poems with a focus on Christmas and the winter solstice, even as I sweated it out in the troubling heatwave of the summer of 2022. I want to express my gratitude to those poets who generously granted permission for new work to be included here: Neil Curry, John Greening, Jeremy Hooker, Denise Saul, Joan Michelson, Penelope Shuttle and Marvin

Thompson. Many thanks also to those authors and publishers who gave permission for the inclusion of work already published (in order of appearance in this anthology): 'The Heart-in-Waiting' by Kevin Crossley-Holland, from *The Mountains of Norfolk: New and Selected Poems* (Enitharmon Press, 2011); 'St Ita's Lullaby' by James Harpur, from *Light Unlocked: Christmas Card Poems*, eds. Crossley-Holland & Sail (Enitharmon Press, 2005) – this lullaby has been set to music by Nicola Lefanu; 'The adoration of the kings' by Martyn Crucefix, first published in *Spring of the Muses: the poetry of music, art and dance*, ed. Deborah Gaye (Avalanche Books, 2019); 'Her Dream at Christmas' by Martyn Crucefix, from *Beneath Tremendous Rain* (Enitharmon Press, 1990); 'Cento' by Kate Bingham, from *Infragreen* (Seren Books, 2015); 'Christmas Cards' by Lotte Kramer, from *More New and Collected Poems* (Rockingham Press, 2015); 'Enter the theologians' by Rishi Dastidar, first published at Visual Verse https://visualverse.org/about-visual-verse/; 'The Circuit' by John Mole, from *Counting the Chimes: New and Selected Poems 1975-2003* (Peterloo Poets, 2004); 'Supply' by Martyn Crucefix, from *Hurt* (Enitharmon Press, 2010); 'Lights' by Nancy Campbell, from *Uneasy Pieces* (Guillemot Press, 2022).

Martyn Crucefix

The Editors

Michael Glover is a Sheffield-born, Cambridge-educated poet and art critic who has written regularly for The *Independent, The Economist, The Times,* the *Financial Times,* the *New Statesman* and the *Tablet.* His books include *Great Works: Encounters with Art* (2016), *Neo Rauch* (2017), *John Ruskin: A Dictionary* (2019), *The Trapper* (2020), *Thrust: a spasmodic pictorial history of the cod-piece in art* (2020), *Nellie's Devils* (2022) and *The Timely Lift-Off of the Famous Harlequin Fish* (2022). He lives in Clapham, South London.

Martyn Crucefix's recent publications include *Cargo of Limbs* (Hercules Editions, 2019) and *The Lovely Disciplines* (Seren, 2017). *These Numbered Days,* translations of poems by Peter Huchel (Shearsman, 2019) won the Schlegel-Tieck Translation Prize, 2020. A Rilke *Selected* is forthcoming from Pushkin Press in 2023 and a translation of Lutz Seiler's essays, *Sundays I Thought of God* will be published by And Other Stories. Currently Royal Literary Fund Fellow at The British Library, Martyn blogs on poetry, translation and teaching at: http://www.martyncrucefix.com

Lightning Source UK Ltd.
Milton Keynes UK
UKHW031447181022
410673UK00001B/113